D1314975

Happy to Be Me!

A Kid's Book About Self-esteem

Written by
Christine Adams and Robert J. Butch

Illustrated by
R. W. Alley

ONE CARING PLACE

Abbey Press
St. Meinrad, IN 47577

For the young children in our lives:

Harrison Edward Hanley
Benjamin Michael Firsick
James Elliot Firsick
Daryl James McKenna
and
Diana Mary Butch

First hardcover edition 2010

Text © 2001 Christine Adams and Robert J. Butch
Illustrations © 2001 St. Meinrad Archabbey
Published by One Caring Place
Abbey Press
St. Meinrad, Indiana 47577

Library of Congress Catalog Number
2001093034

ISBN 978-0-87029-441-9

Printed in the United States of America

A Message to Parents, Teachers, and Other Caring Adults

Experts say a child's self-esteem is the best predictor of her future—whether she will make good choices as a teen, have fulfilling relationships, and become a well-adjusted adult.

How, then, can we "give" children self-esteem? In reality, self-esteem is not some magical substance we can pour into a child. It's not about having an abundance of talent, intelligence, or beauty. In fact, it's not about "having" anything at all. Instilling self-esteem in children means helping them be themselves. We must let them know how loved and cherished they are—for their sheer existence. We must help them find their own special place and purpose in the universe.

Children are works in progress. In the first few years of life, they learn to deal with separation anxiety, shame, self-doubt, and guilt. They desire to mimic the adult world even as they are fighting for their own self-reliance. They encounter sibling rivalry and competition. If adults affirm and love them during this early time, through both successes and mistakes, they will come to believe they are lovable. Later, as children become more socially aware, they develop the skills to gain independence, to get along with peers, to act out of their own burgeoning sense of morality.

All children, of every age, need to be told they are loved and always will be, no matter what they do or don't do. Let each child know he is special, just by being who he is. Help him to discover and develop his gifts at his own pace.

What are some practical things we can suggest to children to enhance self-esteem? Emphasize the idea of being your own best friend, especially through positive self-talk. Show children how to recognize and handle bad days and mistakes. "Catch" them doing something right. Affirm them for their efforts.

Through this book, you can remind the children in your care that they are precious...unique...awesome...even magnificent! And through your ongoing words and actions, you can bring to life God's infinite love for every child.

—Christine Adams and Robert J. Butch

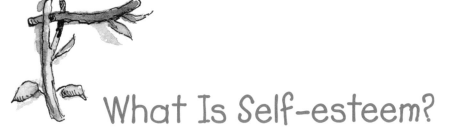

What Is Self-esteem?

"Self-esteem" means how you feel about yourself.

Good self-esteem is a feeling inside that reminds you every day, "I am loved. I am good. I am happy to be me." Good self-esteem means knowing you are a wonderful person—because God made you that way.

You don't have to be the fastest or smartest or best-looking kid to have good self-esteem. You're a star just the way you are!

Who Are You?

You have a first, middle, and last name. You have a certain kind of hair, skin, eyes, and smile. You are good at some things and not as good at other things.

People may say, "You seem like a very nice girl." Or, "What a polite boy!" Or, "You're really good at that." Sometimes people may say things about you that are not so nice. But the words people say about you are not who you are.

So who are you, really? You are a special child of God. You are someone who deserves to be loved. And you *are* loved—by God, by your parents, and by many other people.

Everyone Is Different—and Special!

If you put ink on your finger and press it on a paper, it will make a certain pattern. No one else in the whole world can make that same fingerprint.

There's only one YOU. You don't need to *do* anything special to be special—you already *are*!

Every child is different. Kids come in all kinds of colors, shapes, and sizes. Some kids speak English. Some speak Spanish. Some speak Chinese. Some kids use sign language. God gives each one special love.

You Are a Gift to the World

Everyone has special gifts to bring to the world.

James is good at making people laugh. Alisha knows just the right thing to say when someone is sad. Luis can fix things that are broken. Jameel helps collect money for the homeless. Renee draws beautiful pictures. Other kids look to Chris to help settle arguments during kickball.

The world needs all kinds of people with all kinds of gifts: helpers, fixers, peacemakers, artists. What special gifts do you have to give the world?

Be Your Own Best Self

There may be times when you are not glad to be you. You might even want to be someone else.

Maybe you wish you could play soccer like Harrison, sing like Kathleen, or do math like Ben. Maybe you feel like your dad or mom wants you to be "the best" in something, but you just can't seem to get it.

No one is the best in everything. Some kids can do math but can't play soccer. Some can play soccer but can't sing. Some can sing but can't do math. You have special gifts that God gave you.

Be Your Own Best Friend

You can be your own best friend by taking good care of yourself.

You can eat good food and stay away from things that are bad for your body. You can wear a bike helmet. You can be sure not to play with dangerous things or in dangerous places.

When you are your own best friend, you ignore the voice inside you that may say, "I can't do this because I'm not good enough." You tell yourself instead, "I can do this. I am smart enough to try by myself or ask for help."

Be a Friend to Others

You can make others feel special by being a good friend. Try to share and take turns. If you see a kid learning how to ride a bike, tell him, "Good job!"

Try to remember people's names and say, "Hi." It also makes people feel special when you say, "Please," "Thank you," and "Excuse me." It makes the teacher feel special when you follow the rules and listen in class.

Every day try to do something kind for someone else. For example, if you see a classmate sitting alone on Parent's Day, ask her to sit with you and your mom or dad.

When Things Change

If you have a big change in your life, it can make you wonder whether you are still special and loved.

If you get a new baby brother, for example, lots of people may give him presents. You might wonder if he is going to take your special place in the family.

Talk to your parents about this. They love you just because you're you. No one else could ever take your place.

If someone close to you has to go away, you are still very special to that person. Maybe you can write, phone, or e-mail to stay in touch. You can think about each other during the day and say a little prayer.

Loving Your Family

When your mom gets busy, you can offer to feed the baby. If your dad is too tired to play ball, you can decide not to bug him. Maybe you could teach your younger sister how to tie her shoe.

Sometimes you might feel like your parents treat your brother or sister better than you. Maybe your brother gets to stay up later. Or you got yelled at for something your sister did.

Tell your parents how you feel. They will let you know how much they love you and how special you are. Your parents have enough love for everyone in your family.

Making Mistakes

Everybody makes mistakes. You might want to win a game so much that you add extra points to your score. You might take your little sister's toy, or get mad and yell at your friends.

Be honest about mistakes and say, "I'm sorry," right away. Try to make up for what you did wrong. Remember, God loves you even when you make a mistake. Forgive yourself as God does.

You can also get mad at yourself—like when you can't learn a new game. Slow down and take a deep breath. Go over the rules again or ask for help. If you still can't get it, do something else for awhile and go back to the game later.

Having a Bad Day

Everyone has a bad day sometimes. Maybe you feel tired and crabby. Or you have eight mistakes on your spelling paper, and you miss a soccer goal.

It can help just to say out loud, "I'm having a bad day." Ask someone for a hug. Tell yourself, "I'm still a good kid, even on a bad day."

Try to figure out why this day is so bad. Did you forget to study your spelling words? Next week, you can do better. Give yourself a pat on the back for at least trying to make the soccer goal.

Remember days that were better—like the day you caught your first fish with your grandpa. Remember the hug your mom gave you this morning.

Be True to You

It's good to be yourself, even if you think or feel differently from others. It's good to be true to YOU.

If someone tells you that your art project is weird, but it looks good to you, don't worry about it. People see things differently and have different ideas. That's okay.

If some kids want you to do something wrong, you don't have to do it. Be true to your own feelings, even if others tease you.

Stick Up for Yourself

If someone is mean to you, it's fine to stick up for yourself. Tell her you don't like to be treated that way.

If she keeps on bothering you, don't pay attention. If you need to, tell an adult. Play with friends that make you feel good and special—because you *are*!

If you feel someone is treating you unfairly—even a grownup—tell that person calmly. When someone is mad at you, listen to what he is saying. Try to understand his feelings. Try to work out the problem together.

You've Come a Long Way

When you were a baby, you crawled on the floor. Now you can walk and run and hop and skip. You have learned to play, share, and wait your turn. You have learned about colors and letters and numbers. That's terrific!

Today you have learned how special you are. There is no one else exactly like you. You were born because God knew the world needed someone just like you. Your friends and family love you, because you're YOU.

You can say to yourself proudly, "I am loved. I am good. I am happy to be me!"

Christine A. Adams, M.A., spent thirty-two years teaching and counseling teens. She is the author of two Elf-help titles, *One-day-at-a-time Therapy* and *Gratitude Therapy*. Her other books include *Living In Love* (Health Communications) and *Holy Relationships* (Morehouse Publishing Group). She has three grown children and three grandchildren who live in California, Connecticut, and Massachusetts. Christine is married to co-author, Robert J. Butch.

After a successful business career of thirty years, **Robert J. Butch**, LCSW, earned an MSW degree and turned to counseling, with an emphasis on child and family issues. He practices at the Harbor Schools in Newburyport, Massachusetts. He has three grown sons who live in California, Colorado, and Connecticut. Robert and Christine reside in Maine.

R. W. Alley is the illustrator for the popular Abbey Press adult and children's series of Elf-help books, as well as an illustrator and writer of other children's books. He lives in Barrington, Rhode Island, with his wife, daughter, and son. See a wide variety of his works at: www.rwalley.com.